Contents

Words printed in **bold** in the main text are explained in the glossary on page 45.

Animals in danger

In **Madagascar**, if you get up early in the morning, you will hear strange voices howling in the rainforest. The voices belong to indris, which are a type of lemur. They are waking up, and beginning to feed. They eat leaves and fruit from the trees.

Later on, you will hear the sound of someone chopping wood. Soon smoke rises in the forest.

▼ *An indri sitting in a tall tree.*

The people are cutting down trees and burning them to make room to grow food. People have been doing this in Madagascar for two thousand years. Now almost all the forest has gone, and many lemurs have nowhere to live.

In this book, you can find out about wild animals in danger, and what is being done to help them.

▲ *Some forest has been cleared to grow* **crops**.

▲ *Once these hills in Madagascar were covered in trees.*

The rarest animals in the world

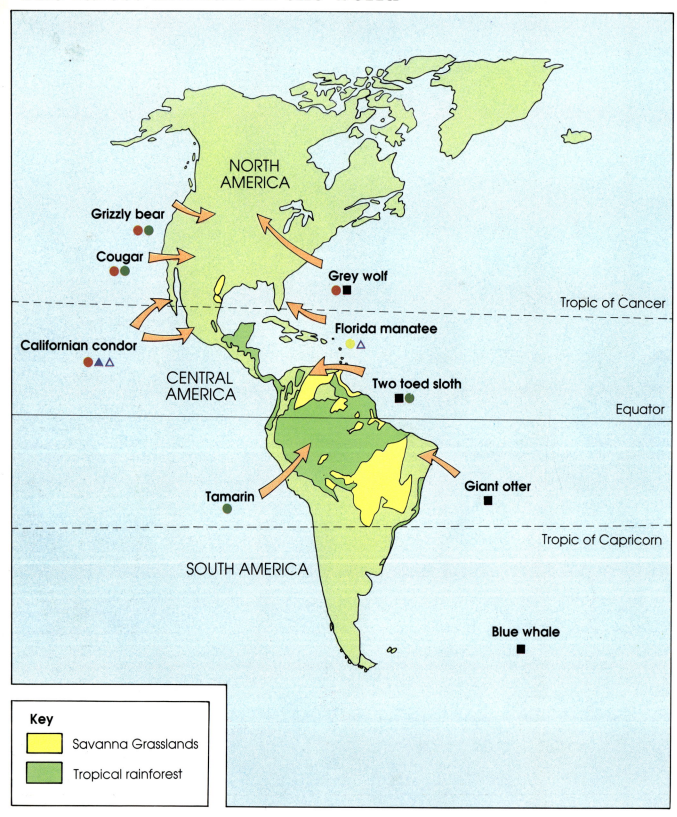

NORTH AMERICA

Grizzly bear

Cougar

Grey wolf

Tropic of Cancer

Florida manatee

Californian condor

CENTRAL AMERICA

Two toed sloth

Equator

Giant otter

Tamarin

Tropic of Capricorn

SOUTH AMERICA

Blue whale

Key

Savanna Grasslands

Tropical rainforest

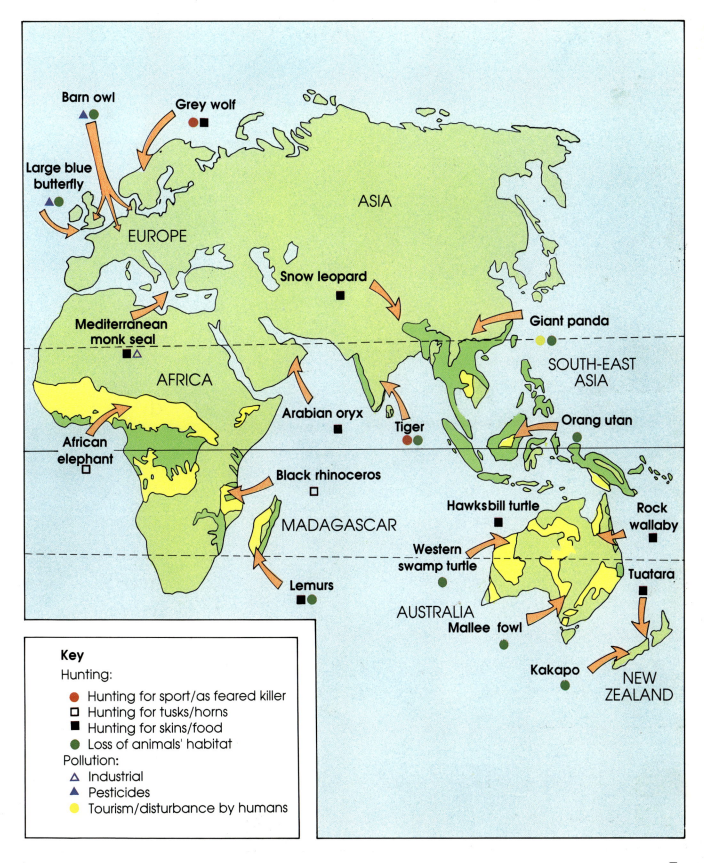

Barn owl

Grey wolf

Large blue butterfly

ASIA

EUROPE

Snow leopard

Giant panda

Mediterranean monk seal

SOUTH-EAST ASIA

AFRICA

Arabian oryx

Orang utan

Tiger

African elephant

Black rhinoceros

Hawksbill turtle

Rock wallaby

MADAGASCAR

Western swamp turtle

Tuatara

AUSTRALIA

Lemurs

Mallee fowl

Kakapo

NEW ZEALAND

Key

Hunting:
- 🔴 Hunting for sport/as feared killer
- ◻ Hunting for tusks/horns
- ◼ Hunting for skins/food
- 🟢 Loss of animals' habitat

Pollution:
- △ Industrial
- ▲ Pesticides
- 🟡 Tourism/disturbance by humans

Animals are in great danger if they lose their forest homes. Forests are being cut down all over the world and many of these are rainforests.

◄ *Rainforests grow in warm, wet countries. Lots of animals live in them.*

There are chimpanzees and sunbirds in African rainforests. Tigers and peacocks live in the Indian rainforest, and jaguars and parrots in South America. Everywhere there are snakes, tree frogs and insects.

Golden toads in the rainforest of Central America. ▶

If the rainforest is cut down, there is nowhere for all these animals to live. Already nearly half the rainforests in the world have gone.

There are fewer than 4,000 orang-utans left in the world. This is because their rainforest homes have been cut down.

▲ *Orang-utans hanging from trees in the rainforest.*

◄ *This small monkey, called an emperor tamarin, lives in the forests of the River Amazon in South America.*

Trees are not only useful as homes for animals. Their roots hold the soil in place. When the trees have gone, the rain will soon wash the soil away. This is called **erosion**.

The rainwater makes channels in the ground as it carries the soil down to rivers and then to the sea. The soil settles near the river mouth, blocking it. This may cause flooding.

▲ *This flood in Bangladesh was caused by the cutting down of forests on mountain slopes far away.*

◄ *People living on the slopes of the **Himalayas** make **terraces** to stop the soil being washed away.*

▲ *Once there were millions of bison in North America. Now there are only a few left.*

People need land to grow food. Often they spray the land with weedkiller. They put up fences and wild animals like deer and buffalo can no longer search about for food. Insects, and the birds which eat them, have nowhere to live when all the weeds are killed.

▲ *Beautiful plants like marsh marigolds grow in wet places.*

Many animals live in ponds and **marshes**. Often these are drained to make farmland. When the rivers and river banks are cleared, the animals living among the reeds or water weed have nowhere to go. Marshes provide food for many birds, but farmers drain the marshes to grow their crops.

Saving the whooping crane

Whooping cranes live in North America. When people from Europe went there, they drove the birds away from the marshes where they used to rest and feed. The marshes were drained and turned into farmland, and many of the cranes were shot. Fifty years ago there were only 15 cranes left.

The cranes' summer breeding place in Canada is carefully protected. In winter they fly south to Texas, in the USA, where it is warmer. They are protected there, too. Now there are nearly 100 cranes, and their numbers are increasing. But they are still not safe from oil and chemicals that could spill from ships and **pollute** the marshes where they live.

▼ *Whooping cranes in their winter home in Texas.*

Hunting and killing

▲ *In this picture you can see puffins, kittiwakes and shags. They all feed on the same fish that humans eat.*

People have always killed animals to eat. Some people, like the Indians by the River Amazon, or Bushmen in Africa, still go out hunting for their food. Most people now eat animals that have been raised on farms, but many wild animals are still killed by hunters. Most of the wild animals killed every year are fish. In some places, so many are caught that there may soon be none left.

Most types of whales have become very **rare** because they were hunted so much in the past. There is no need to kill whales for their meat and oil any more, and most countries have now given up killing them.

How many whales are left?

Name of whale	Numbers today	Numbers before whaling
Blue	1,000-5,000	500,000
Humpback	1,000-3,000	300,000
Greenland right	3,800	20,000
Sperm	950,000	unknown
Fin	80,000	unknown

(These are estimated figures)

▼ *Fewer whales are now killed.*

15

Some people enjoy hunting and killing animals for sport. Not long ago, someone who went to Africa to kill a lion, or to India to kill a tiger, was thought to be very brave.

▼ *People gather at the start of a fox hunt to protest against it.*

▲ *A black bear, safe in a national park in the USA.*

Today, many people think that hunting for sport is cruel, but it still goes on in many countries. Some animals are killed because people fear them. Some people think animals should be left alone, and humans should keep out of their way.

Many animals are protected because they are rare.

Some people kill protected animals to get money. They are called **poachers**. They hunt cheetahs and leopards for their beautiful skins, which are made into clothes. Poachers also hunt rhinos and sell their horns. In some countries the horns are used for medicine.

▲ *Some people still wear coats made of animal skins.*

Snow leopards are very rare.
▼

▲ *There are only 30 white rhinos left in Kenya. These are six of them.*

How many rhinos are left?

Some types of rhino are very rare. There are now very few Javan rhinos living in the islands of Java and Sumatra, in Asia. In South Africa, white rhinos are carefully protected and their numbers are increasing. But black rhinos, which used to range all over Africa, are now becoming much rarer because so many have been killed. The few that are left live mostly in the southern part of the continent.

Pollution

Smoke from burning coal or wood causes air pollution. Burning anything makes a gas called carbon dioxide. This gas collects in a layer high in the air. It stops heat escaping into space. The Earth is gradually getting warmer because the layer of carbon dioxide in the sky is getting thicker. Acid gases in the air form **acid rain** which kills fish in lakes and rivers, and damages trees.

▼ *Steam from power stations is harmless, but acid gases from the fuel they burn is harmful.*

▲ **Radiation** *from an explosion at a nuclear power station harmed reindeer living far away from the explosion.*

Old-style aerosols, refrigerators, and hamburger boxes contain gases called CFCs. When the fridge or aerosol is thrown away, the gases drift up into the sky. There they harm the **ozone layer**. The ozone layer prevents too much **ultraviolet light** from the sun reaching Earth. If the ozone layer is damaged, the Earth will get too hot.

The sea is getting more and more polluted by oil and other chemicals. These cause great harm to fish and birds.

Some chemicals used in factories cause pollution that is even more dangerous than oil. Used chemicals should be burned, but this costs a lot of money. To save money, the chemicals are sometimes buried underground, or allowed to flow down rivers and into the sea. They can harm the animals that live there.

▼ *This penguin's feathers were clogged with oil.*

Pesticides are chemicals used on farms to kill weeds and harmful insects. They often kill other plants and animals as well.

If a mouse eats wheat which has been treated with a pesticide, the mouse might become poisonous. When an owl eats the mouse, the poison will harm the owl and its babies.

This harvest mouse is building its nest. Many harvest mice have been harmed by pesticides. ▼

▼ *Members of Greenpeace, a **conservation group**, complain about oil being dumped in the sea.*

23

Safe places for animals

A national park is a large area of land which is protected from harm. People can visit the park to look at plants and animals that no longer **survive** in other parts of the country. The first national park in the world was at Yellowstone, in the USA. It was opened in 1872. Over a hundred years later, it is a safe home for buffalo, elk, grizzly bears, and many other animals.

▼ *Ibex live safely in the Gran Paradiso National Park in Italy.*

Tigers had become very rare in India because people used to hunt them for sport. The World Wide Fund for Nature drew up a plan called Project Tiger, to save them. Eight parks were set up in India where tigers would be safe. When the project started, there were only 2,000 tigers in India. After the first ten years, there were over 4,000. Now tigers seem to be safe.

Now most countries have national parks. People from other countries come to visit them, to see the animals and the beautiful scenery protected in the park. The visitors pay money to go in. The money helps the people who live in the country as well as saving the animals.

▲ *Millions of water birds live in the swamps of the Everglades.*

Not all national parks are safe. The Everglades is a huge park in Florida, USA. It is mostly **swamp**. Farmers take the water for their crops, and people living near the park use it for drinking and washing. The Everglades is becoming very dry.

▲ *Visitors watch animals at a park in Nepal.*

Some of the water flowing into the swamp from the farms is polluted. If the Everglades is not saved, millions of birds, snakes and alligators will die.

Some people think that national parks are too like big zoos. Others think all zoos are wrong, because animals should be free. But some animals only survive in zoos.

This black rhino mother and calf have been rescued from poachers and given a new home in a national park. ▼

Saving animals in zoos

People like to go to the zoo, to see the animals and to learn about them.

In the past, all zoo animals were captured by hunters and brought to the zoo. If animals are born in a zoo, no more animals of that kind need to be captured.

▼ *Animals like this hippo are safe in the zoo.*

▲ *The special herd of Arabian oryx in Arizona, USA.*

When there are enough of them, some can be set free where they used to live.

Once, all the wild Arabian oryx had been killed by hunters, but there were some that were safe in zoos. All the oryx in all the zoos in the world were collected together to make one **herd**. When their babies were born, some of the oryx were taken back to their home and set free in the desert where they used to live.

Another famous animal that was saved by breeding in zoos is the Hawaiian goose. Once there were only thirty of these geese left in Hawaii. The bushes where they lived had been eaten by cattle and goats, and the geese had been killed by dogs and cats. To save them, some were captured and brought to England. They soon produced plenty of eggs and **goslings**. Soon a few hundred had been sent back to Hawaii, where they are now protected.

▲ *This female eland is looking after a baby bongo, a very rare African animal.*

These Hawaiian geese live at a Wildfowl Trust in England. ▶

Woolly Monkeys

Woolly monkeys come from South America. Many of them have no homes, because their forest has been cut down. People feel sorry for them, and take them away to live in zoos. But if we can save enough rainforest, we could let the monkeys go free again.

This woolly monkey lives in safety at a sanctuary in Cornwall, England. ▶

Changing how people think

The best way to save wildlife is to change the way people think. When people see a woolly monkey, they begin to think of ways to save its home in the rainforest. If people in the Far East did not think rhino horns made good medicine, poachers would not kill rhinos.

A lot of people today want to buy **organic food**, so that farmers do not have to use pesticides and fertilizers that damage wildlife. Many of the dangerous chemicals which were once used in factories have been banned.

▼ *Organic farmers do not use sprays to kill pests and weeds.*

▲ *Heavy machines squash and ruin the soft soil where the rainforest once stood.*

Burning coal and oil to make electricity pollutes the air, but now there are new ways of making electricity, without burning coal or oil.

Cutting down rainforest trees need not ruin the land. If people did not use heavy machines, the soft forest soil would last longer and grow better crops.

In many Mediterranean countries people shoot small songbirds. People in the Faeroe Islands, in the North Atlantic, kill pilot whales. In Texas, they hunt and kill rattlesnakes. Although some of the animals are eaten, these people do not need the meat. The killing is done because it has always been the custom, or **tradition**.

The Californian condor

The Californian condor is a very big bird. It produces a chick only once every three years. So many condors have been killed, by hunting or poisoning, that there are only a very few left. Soon there will be none left at all. The Californian condor will then be **extinct**.

Perhaps when today's children grow up they will no longer kill animals just because their parents did.

These pilot whales in the Faeroe Islands were driven on to a beach and killed. ▼

People need land for farms, roads and homes. But animals need land too. ▼

The main problem today is that there are too many people in the world. In the past, most children died before they grew up. Today, most survive, so there is no need to have big families. People need to change the way they think about some of their traditions, such as hunting and having lots of children.

▼ *Chimpanzees may be used to test medicines for humans.*

Looking ahead

Not all the news about wildlife is bad news. We have seen how the Arabian oryx and the Hawaiian goose were saved. The people who saved them belonged to two **charities**, the Fauna and Flora Preservation Society, and the Wildfowl and Wetlands Trust. Anyone can join. The World Wide Fund for Nature (WWF) works to save wildlife all over the world. Other organizations are trying to stop the buying and selling of rhino horns, and ivory from elephant tusks.

▼ *People in Papua New Guinea, in South-East Asia, used to kill birds of paradise to make headdresses.*

Saving possums in Australia

A tiny possum which lives in Australia has been saved by a tunnel. The males and the females live on different parts of a mountain. A new road separates the two places. When the males tried to visit the females, they were killed by cars. The WWF suggested building a tunnel so that the males could cross the road safely. It worked, and now the males and females can meet safely and produce young.

In Papua new Guinea, the local people once killed birds of paradise for their feathers. Now they protect them. They have made **hides** where visitors can sit to watch the beautiful birds.

In Mexico, farmers used to cut down the trees where monarch butterflies spend the winter. Now they protect the trees, so that visitors can see the butterflies.

Monarch butterflies are welcomed in California. ▼

Travellers bring back stories and photographs from their holidays of the wonderful birds, animals and insects they have seen. Sometimes these stories encourage us to give money to help to save the wildlife far away.

▼ *Looking after a kakapo, a rare parrot in New Zealand. Kakapos cannot fly.*

▲ *A pair of Large Blue butterflies feed on a plant called wild thyme.*

Saving a rare butterfly in Britain

When they are caterpillars, Large Blue butterflies live inside ants' nests. The ants look after the caterpillar until it turns into a butterfly. All the Large Blue butterflies had died out in Britain because of the chemicals used on farmland. Then some caterpillars of the Large Blue butterfly were brought over to Britain from Sweden and set free in a safe place. When they grew into butterflies, they laid eggs. The ants looked after the caterpillars when the eggs hatched. Now the Large Blue butterfly is safe in Britain once more.

This book started in Madagascar. People there are chopping down the forests where the lemurs live. The good news is that there is now a plan to save some of the forests, and the lemurs that live in them. One lemur, called the aye-aye, was taken to a small island where it would be safe. Nine aye-ayes went to the island, and there are now about fifty of them. Other lemurs are now protected in special parts of the forest.

▼ *An aye-aye can bite into green coconuts to drink the juice.*

Madagascar: island of the lemurs

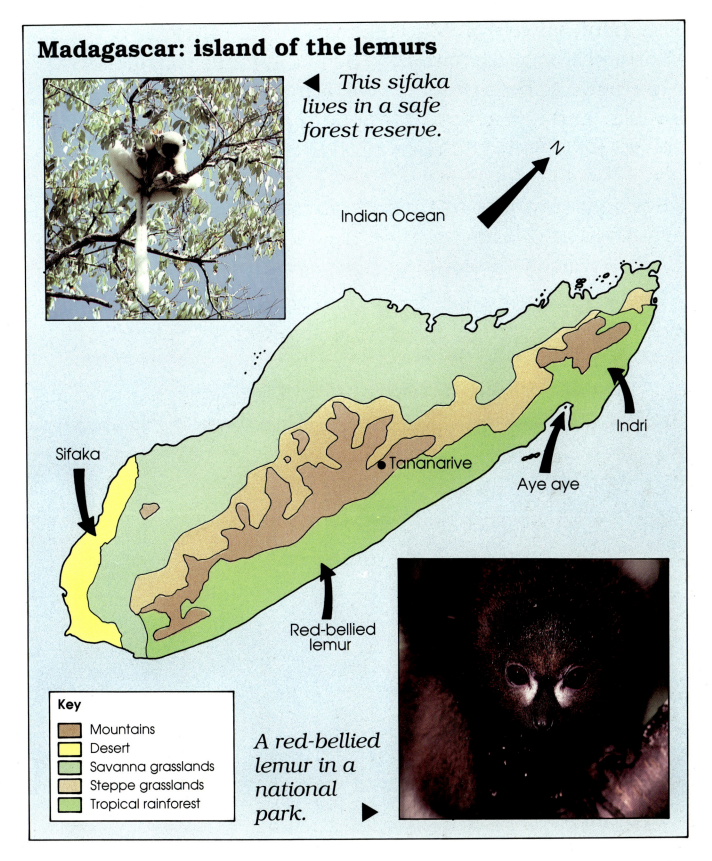

◄ *This sifaka lives in a safe forest reserve.*

N

Indian Ocean

Sifaka

Tananarive

Indri

Aye aye

Red-bellied lemur

Key

- ▨ Mountains
- ▨ Desert
- ▨ Savanna grasslands
- ▨ Steppe grasslands
- ▨ Tropical rainforest

A red-bellied lemur in a national park. ►

What you can do

To help to save wildlife, you could join one of the conservation groups in the list at the back of this book. You have already heard of WWF and its work all over the world. If you like birds, you could join the Royal Society for the Protection of Birds (RSPB).

Greenpeace works to save rainforests, and to stop pollution and hunting in many parts of the world. You can protect wildlife yourself, too, by being careful not to cause any damage when you go for a walk in the country. Look but don't touch.

▼ *A baby seal being looked after at a seal orphanage in Holland.*

How to make your own nature reserve

Here are some clues. Butterflies love to feed at a bush called Buddleia. Many of them lay their eggs on nettles. Their caterpillars eat the leaves. Bumblebees like foxgloves. Frogs, water beetles, and dragonflies will come to live in a small pond. Birds soon come to feed at a bird table or balcony if you put food out regularly.

▼ *In Australia some farmers kill grey kangaroos. These kangaroos are safe from farmers and have become very tame.*

Eight things to do
* Tell people why it is harmful to use pesticides and weedkillers.
* Do not leave litter. It can be dangerous to animals.
* Visit your nearest nature reserve.
* Join a conservation group.
* Learn the names of the birds, insects and flowers which you see around you.
* Make a wildlife corner in your own, or your school garden.
* Tell your parents or your teacher if you think there may be animals or plants being harmed nearby.
* Remember that all creatures have a right to live.

Making a wildlife garden

Some wild flowers are good for wildlife. Butterflies feed at thistle flowers, and goldfinches eat the seeds. Bees like clover, poppies, and bluebells. Plant wild flower seeds in a corner with other weeds. They will make seeds so that there will be more wild flowers next year.

Glossary

Acid rain   Rainwater polluted by gases in the air.

Charity   A group of people who collect money for a good cause.

Crops   Plants grown for food.

Conservation group   A group of people who work to protect animals and plants and the places where they live.

Erosion   Soil being washed away by water, or blown away by wind.

Extinct   No longer found anywhere in the world.

Gosling   A young goose.

Herd   A group of large animals such as cows or oryx.

Hide   A hidden shelter where people go to watch animals and birds without disturbing them.

Himalayas   A mountain range in Southern Asia, the highest in the world.

Madagascar   A large tropical island off the eastern coast of Africa.

Marshes   Low-lying, wet land.

Organic food   Food which is grown without using chemicals.

Ozone layer   A layer of gas in the sky which reduces the amount of ultraviolet light reaching the ground.

Pesticide   A chemical used for killing insects that destroy crops.

Poacher   Someone who kills protected animals.

Pollute   To harm the air or water or land by human activity.

Radiation   Dangerous rays produced by the fuel in nuclear power stations.

Rainforest   Forest that grows in warm, wet countries.

Rare   An animal is rare when there are not many of them left.

Survive   Stay alive.

Swamp   A wet, muddy place with trees and ponds.

Terraces   Wide steps cut into a hillside where crops are grown.

Tradition   Something which people have done for a long time without thinking why they do it.

Ultraviolet light   The harmful part of sunlight.

Finding out more

Books to read

Jungles   by Angela Wilkes (Usborne, 1990)
Life in the Rainforests   by Lucy Baker (Franklin Watts, 1990)
Monkeys (Wildlife at Risk)   by Tess Lemmon (Wayland, 1991)
Pandas (Wildlife at Risk)   by Gill Standring (Wayland, 1991)
Tigers (Wildlife at Risk)   by Helen Riley (Wayland, 1990)
Rhinos (Wildlife at Risk)   by Malcolm Penny (Wayland, 1991)

Useful addresses

Australian Association for
  Environmental Education
GPO Box 112
Canberra ACT 2601

Environment and
  Conservation
  Organizations of New
  Zealand (ECO)
P.O. Box 11057
Wellington

Friends of the Earth (UK)
26-28 Underwood Street
London N1 7JQ

Friends of the Earth
  (Australia)
National Liaison Office
366 Smith Street
Collingwood
Victoria 3065

Friends of the Earth (Canada)
Suite 53-54
Queen Street
Ottawa KP5CS

Friends of the Earth (NZ)
Nagal House
Courthouse Lane
PO Box 39/065
Auckland West

Greenpeace (UK)
30-31 Islington Green
London N1 8XE

Greenpeace (USA)
1611 Connecticut Avenue N.W.
Washington DC2009

Greenpeace (Australia)
310 Angas Street
Adelaide 5000

Greenpeace (Canada)
2623 West 4th Avenue
Vancouver BCV6K 1P8

The Royal Society for the
  Protection of Birds
The Lodge
Sandy
Bedfordshire SG19 2DL

Watch
22 The Green
Nettleham
Lincs LN2 2NR
England

World Wide Fund for Nature
WWF Information and
  Education Division
1196 Gland
Switzerland

Index

Picture acknowledgements
The publishers would like to thank the following for allowing their photographs to be reproduced in his book:
Bryan and Cherry Alexander 21; Ardea London Ltd 40 (Liz and Tony Bomford); Bruce Coleman Ltd 4 and 41 below (O.Langrand), 8 below and 33 (L.C. Marigo), 9 above and 22 (Gerald Cubitt), 9 below (Dieter and Mary Plage), 11,17 and 34 (Jeff Foott), 13 (Joy Langsbury), 14 (John Markham), 19 (Christian Zuber), 20 (Robert Carr), 26 above (Erwin and Peggy Bauer), 28 (Francisco Futil), 29 (Jen and Des Bartlett), 30 below (Gordon Langsbury), 35 above (Bruce Coleman), 35 below (Helmut Albrecht), 36 (Huli Wigmen); Environmental Investigation Agency 34 (Dave Currey); Frank Lane 30 above (Ron Austing), 31 (Frank W Lane); Greenpeace 23 below (Morgan) 42 (Dorreboom); ICCE 6 (Sue Wells), 8 above (John Mackinnon); Oxford Scientific Films 5 above and 41 above (Mark Pidgeon), 5 below (David Curl), 7 (Michael Fogden), 16 (Anna Walsh), 18 below (Michael Dick), 19 (Mike Birkhead), 23 (Sean Morris); Rex Features 10; Survival Anglia Ltd 12 and 37 (Jeff Foott), 26 below (Dieter Plage), 27 (Jen and Des Bartlett), 38 (Annie Price), 39 (Dennis Green); ZEFA 15 (K. Scholz), 24, 43 (P.Blok). Cover: Bruce Coleman.
The illustrations are by Marilyn Clay.